Crucify Me Gently

Hilary Nili

NEWMAN SPRINGS PUBLISHING
320 Broad Street
Red Bank, NJ 07701

First originally published by Newman Springs Publishing 2024

ISBN 979-8-89308-457-3 (Paperback)
ISBN 979-8-89308-458-0 (Digital)

Printed in the United States of America

For all those in the system

Acknowledgments

My deepest thanks to
Ali Chabot, Kerry Gagniere, and Marlena Siegel

Klonopin 2 Milligrams

Klonopin raging through my system.
Multiple panic attacks.
Feeling overwhelmed.
Let me die.

Klonopin
Dulling my senses.
Making me second-guess my every move.
Let me go.
There are no options.

3:00 p.m. wondering if life goes on.

I take another Klonopin and sink into a daze.
Let me die.

Treasures

All the beloved treasures were taken away like rose petals dying.
My father made everything become dust and ashes.

Look beneath a tombstone for buried possessions from another life.

I whisper in the night,
Let me hold one more time my memories.

Instead, I remember the destruction and the despair.
Remember the roses.
Remember them well.

Dead End

The lithium, the Trilafon, and the Risperdal flatline me.
Three antipsychotics and I am a shadow.

Months go by.
I cannot remember the days.
Can I beg?
I'll pay you for a cigarette.

The noose is tight.
The hospital decides on diagnosis and drugs.
One's future is sealed.

A one-act play with no ending.
The lines are written for you.

Taking Chances

I escape from Risperdal, Trilafon, and
lithium with the help of weed.

I get high and take a chance to get off the antipsychotics.
Desperate times call for drastic measures.

A death sentence is averted.
Dr. Berman is a memory, and I am free.

PTSD

My father's voice is in my head.
It says, "Don't turn around, or I'll kill you."
I am eight.
I am in my bed.

The abandoned house is dark.
My father leads me in.
He holds me.
He masturbates.
I am three.

How do you hold back a river of tears?

I am thirty-nine.
The memories awaken.
I am that little girl again.
The unthinkable.
The rape.
The trauma all rise.

Nightmare

I am in high school.
I wake up screaming out of my sleep.

I see in my nightmare an abandoned room with
newspaper balled up and my father's face.

Misdiagnosis

I am in the system for the past thirty years as a schizoaffective.
Once labeled, it sticks.

I am dealt a bad hand,
Playing poker with my life.

Every time I turn to a hospital for help, that label precedes me.

Bad Dream

Banging your head against the wall.
You are a mental patient.
The system owns you.

No matter how many times you come up for air, you are drowning.

Haldol. I gain fifty pounds and lose my period. My skin breaks out.

Akathisia.
The constant motion of your legs pacing for hours.

You beg for relief.
The hospital hotline says to drink tea.

It is a bad dream that owns you.

University Hospital

Tardive dyskinesia. The Haldol becomes toxic.
My tongue and body involuntarily move.
The hospital declares, "We'll take care of you."

A new medication. It takes away my memory.
The hospital proclaims, "We'll help you."
I am back at Mass Mental. I am an inpatient.
Taken off meds to start experimental drugs.
Before that happens, I leave.

After two years, I am off medication. I took care of me.

Pushing Buttons

My father pushes my buttons. He knows how to unhinge me.

I shatter the TV with a cinder block.

I break the glass into a million pieces. My
father controls the moment.
He shatters me into a million pieces.

My Father

He doesn't ask questions.
He just steps on the day.
His agenda beckons to him.

He thinks he is the center of his universe.
There is no God save his own.
He is sacred.
He is untouchable.

He is above reproach.
For he is superior.
He is a doctor.
The Hippocratic oath is a waste of his omnipotence.

He bludgeons life for he can.
He is holy unto himself.
What he destroys is irrelevant.
Now go.
He is the master of the universe.

Commitment

I am at McLean Hospital in Brockton.
I have been here for a month and a half.

Psychosis.
I can translate it.
My father has killed me in my bathroom.

For two weeks I do not sleep.
I am on my guard.
I advocate for myself after centuries of mistakes by hospitals.

In two days, I am to go before a judge for commitment.
Locked away and forgotten for life.

Dr. Williams, a young African American doctor, releases me.
I dodge a bullet.
Life is possible.

The Moment

He goes ballistic.
The kitchen chair becomes a weapon.
No one else is home.

I grab a knife from a drawer. I say, "If you ever
try to hurt me again, I'll kill you."

I never tell my mother about this.
I bury it in the back of my mind
Until now.

A Summer's Night

My father drives to the abandoned house on a summer's night.

He drives there, presenting the abandoned house as a trophy.

He turns on the car's headlights and says,
"Isn't this beautiful real estate?"

My mother, my aunt,
My uncle, my sister, and I all laugh.

If only the property could talk this night.

The Car Mirror

He vainly combs his hair with a cheap black plastic comb.
He never misses his image in the car mirror.

He is a dandy.
Hair plugs cover the receding part of his head.

I say from the back of the car, "You only love yourself."
My mother agrees for the first and last time in her life.

He kisses his hand and says slyly, "I love myself."

The Shot

I get an allergy shot from my father for convenience.
He does not measure the dose.
I observe this.

I go, and soon after there is a thick green
mucus discharge from my nose.
I can't breathe.

I never go back to my father for convenience.

Remembering

I am at Park Street Station in Boston.
I watch the pretty college girls and remember
that was how I once looked.

Now I am a mental patient,
Fifty pounds heavier with acne and akathisia
making my legs move independently.

Now I am okay, but I remember when I was an outsider.
When it was hard to dress and fix my hair on Haldol.

My Teeth

From the dry mouth created by Risperdal,
Lithium, and Trilafon, I get gum disease.

My father proclaims, "You don't need your teeth."

I beg him for the money to save my mouth.

The antibiotic is administered, and I keep my teeth.

Mass General Hospital

I am at Mass General Hospital in Boston
in a psychiatric holding cell.
I am told to undress.
I don't comply.

There is a bucket in the clear cell for a bathroom facility.
I will not use it.

Time passes.
I ask the attendant if I can use the bathroom down the hall.

I return to the holding cell and ask if I can put on lipstick.
A female attendant says, "See, you let her use the
bathroom, and now she thinks she runs the show."

Woods

I am in the woods.
My refuge.
I sit for hours by a stream.
The sound is soothing.

I walk through the woods.
Everything bad disappears.

The cattails grow abundantly.
They touch the sky.

Nothing can hurt me here.
I am safe for the moment.
Maybe I will never go home.
I am safe here.

Drunk

My father is drunk.
He can't hold his liquor. We are at a wedding.
We are at a bar mitzvah.

It doesn't matter the event.
It is always the same.

He dances with me.
In a frenzy, he moves.
His eyes look crazy.
He leans in.
He flashes an inebriated grin.

I dance with him solemnly.
My body is with him.
My mind is somewhere else.

Good Samaritan

I am at Good Samaritan Hospital in
Brockton in the psychiatric unit.

There is a young girl there.
Her johnny is falling off, partially revealing her chest.

I ask her how many medications she's on.
She has no idea.

The guard notices I am wearing a Star of David.
As the nurse injects Zyprexa, the guard says, "I have Jew in me too."

Smoking

I am at Pembroke Hospital. I am thirty-nine,
and I remember my father has raped me.

I want to die.
Remembering, I start to smoke cigarettes, hoping I will get cancer.

I inhale deeply.
Death is my friend.
My father is my enemy.
I choose death today.

Angels

My father says, "I don't care where you go. Live on the street."

I take forty Valium.
I take them one at a time.

I lay in my bed.
Waiting.
Nothing happens.

Angels bless me.

Home Free

My father is paranoid.
He constantly wonders if I will tell him about the rape.
Will I remember?

He is relieved when I am diagnosed as schizoaffective.
He feels home free.

Mass Mental

I am at Mass Mental Hospital in Boston.
When I am admitted, I am asked if I hear voices.
That seals my fate.

It is my first hospitalization.
It is a state facility.
I have no insurance.

I am shelved away with inmates off the street.
We are unclaimed.
We are forgotten.

Downsizing

My father wants to downsize.
He says, "Move out," to me.

I ask where I am supposed to go.
He is screaming on the phone.

An hour later, he calls back.
He lies and says, "I have looked around, and it is
cheaper for you to stay where you are."

Self-Love

I am at McLean Hospital.
The director, Dr. Ridiger, tells me I have no self-worth or self-love.

When I return to see him, I have the head
of nursing with me as my witness.

I say to him, "My mother brought me up
with culture. I had a bat mitzvah."

I leave the good doctor in the dust.
He wants to hang me.

The Kick

My father can't find my sister.
I tell him she is at the high school.

He returns enraged.
He kicks me in the crotch.

I am in my McDonald's uniform.
I say, "You are a madman."

I walk for hours, humiliated and alone.

Lithium

I am at McLean Hospital. I am getting my vitals taken.

The nurse says, "Are you ready to take your lithium?"
I say nothing.

I walk out, and I never have to see that nurse again.

Death

I talk to my father.
Every night, we talk about him, his day, and his activities.
I always end the conversation by saying, "I love you."
This goes on for a year and a half.

On his deathbed, he says, "You are on your own now."

I say nothing.
I hang up the phone.
Only in death am I free.

Crucify Me Gently

Crucify me gently so it doesn't hurt, so I don't feel pain.

Crucify me gently.
Hold me close to your heart so I am not forgotten.

Crucify me gently and remember my
voice, even if it is just a whisper.

Crucify me gently.
Let my body rest in your arms.
Hear my beating heart for an eternity.

Freedom

I survived.
I triumphed over every hurdle.
Never take your freedom for granted.
Freedom is life and love.

I always looked to the far horizon.
I am continually inspired.
I am free.

My journey has taken me to places I could never imagine.

Here I am, but for the grace of God.

The Angel of Mercy

Did you say there is an angel waiting in the wings?
Please spread your wings and
fly to me.

I am in need of healing, and I need your touch.
Fly to me and pray for me.

I saw an angel come to me, saying, "You are safe,
for I see your need; you are safe. For I am here to
comfort you, to surround you with mercy."